COMPANION WORKBOOK
COMPASS
The Journey of the Soul from Egypt to the Promised Land

Penelope V. Yorke

PCS RESOURCES

Publisher: PCS Resources - pcsresource@gmail.com
ISBN (paperback - color): 978-0-9863896-0-3
ISBN (paperback - black and white): 978-0-9863896-4-1
Cover Art and Cover Interior Images: Neil Hague, www.NeilHague.com
Interior Graphic Artist: Chelsea Yarger, chel_seashell@hotmail.com

Contents

Contents

Introduction

This is a *Companion Workbook* to *Compass: The Journey of the Soul from Egypt to the Promised Land.*

I decided to create a workbook to provide a sacred space where you can delve more deeply into the work and lessons learned in each stage of spiritual development. *The Compass Companion Workbook* will help you to determine what stage of spiritual development you are at in the different areas of your life. It will also provide you with an opportunity to observe your conscious and unconscious mind. This will be done as a result of answering the Reflection Questions and by performing Activities that will further engage you in meaningful spiritual work.

You have a space where you can journal about the inner happenings that occur on your journey of the soul. To be able to communicate your experiences through words in each stage of spiritual development will benefit you by making the journey seem more concrete to you.

You will take a journey of the soul more than once in different life areas such as work, relationships, etc. You will learn many lessons that you will later forget when you are in subsequent stages of spiritual development. Lessons that you have forgotten you will have to repeat. Having a journal that chronicles the lessons you learn in each stage of spiritual development will keep you from having to relearn all of them, since you can revisit them here.

I know how most people feel about workbooks—including me: we do not like them. Why? They require us to work! However, you are now aware that you are on a journey of the soul—doing the necessary work to evolve can no longer be delayed. This companion workbook will serve as an internal barometer to your thoughts and feelings to help you evolve.

How to Use This Book

First and foremost, this book is your own personal record of your inner thoughts and emotions. Use this book as a sacred space to do the necessary work to determine where you are on the journey of the soul, and to measure your spiritual growth.

A checklist is provided for every stage of spiritual development to help you determine what stage in the journey you are in. My suggestion is that you fill out the checklists in pencil so that you can reuse these pages in different life areas as your consciousness evolves. The checklist is not a precise measure. Yet what it does give you is a general range of where you are in the journey of the soul, thus pinpointing the appropriate place for you to work in this workbook.

After you determine where you are in consciousness in either one or more life areas, then you are ready to answer the Reflection Questions. The purpose of these questions is to delve into your subconscious and to bring to conscious awareness what lies there. Your subconscious mind is what fuels much of your behavior, so increased awareness will provide you with valuable insights.

Specific activities to help you do further work are given in this workbook. These activities vary in nature and are specific to each stage of spiritual development. Doing them will shift something in you, even if you are not aware of it at the time. Activities pages, both lined and unlined, have been provided for you to use.

The Reflection Questions and the Activities are to be done in your own time frame. However, I suggest that you make a plan for doing them. As such, a weekly planner and a monthly planner have been provided in the Resources section of the workbook. This also gives you a way of reviewing how much time you have spent doing the work necessary for spiritual evolution. There is a connection between how much spiritual work we do and how much we evolve.

How to Use This Book

Having a space where you can record your experiences and what you learn when on your journey is very important. A journal is a window into your soul. A couple of journal pages are provided to facilitate the start of this process. Individual journals for each stage of spiritual development are available for purchase.

Appreciation is another key component to the process of spiritual evolution. When you appreciate what you receive, you attract more of the same into your life. Recording the things that you appreciate helps you to become aware, firstly, of what they are. Secondly, it creates feelings of appreciation within you that attract more in their wake. Appreciation pages for you to complete can be found in the Resources section of the workbook.

Further insight and guidance on each stage of spiritual development has been provided. My intention is for this workbook to help facilitate the work that you need to do in the process of evolving.

Egypt

Select a number between 1 and 7 (with 7 being the highest) that reflects how true each statement is for you presently.

☐ I long to leave the place in which I now find myself.

☐ I am starting to feel resentment about being here.

☐ I no longer feel overwhelming fear about leaving.

☐ I no longer define success based on my material accomplishments.

☐ A sense of increased urgency is spurring me to take action.

☐ My fears make my dreams seem impossible.

☐ I no longer allow the opinions of others to influence me.

☐ I no longer feel debilitating guilt about leaving.

☐ I feel that there has to be more to life than where I am now, and what I have now.

☐ I am starting to lose contact with my soul.

Add the numbers in all of the boxes together, and shade in the total number in the bar graph below. Revisit this activity periodically to gauge your readiness to leave Egypt.

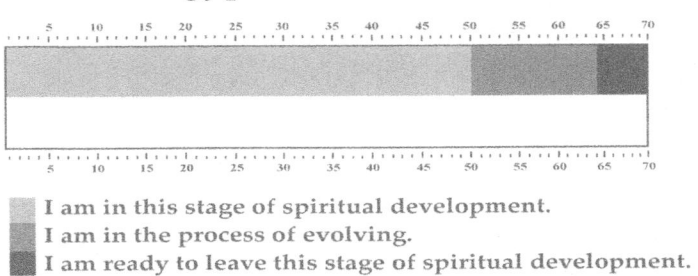

■ I am in this stage of spiritual development.
■ I am in the process of evolving.
■ I am ready to leave this stage of spiritual development.

When you are ready to leave Egypt, you will start a journey that you will be on for the rest of your life: the journey of your soul. Your soul is being asked to leave Egypt - the place of its confinement. Leaving Egypt at first seems too terrifying to consider. Remember your ego is not the one being asked to leave Egypt, your soul is being asked.

Your pharaoh consciousness is now being liberated by Moses. Moses is demanding that you let his people go. His people are the millions of thoughts that you hold in your mind that are now ready to be led by spirit.

People who are ready to leave Egypt have tuned into their soul and are ready to follow its dictates, usually for the first time. An opening has been created through their fears long enough for them to make a change. Saving up some money to help you on the journey may seem like a good idea. Yet however much you save, it will not be enough.

This is because part of your journey in the Wilderness will be becoming dependent on the I Am to provide for you. Your bank account will no longer be your primary means of support. You cannot finance your journey. This is a terrifying thought, but one that gradually needs to be introduced into your consciousness now. It will save you a lot of terror later when the money that you have saved starts to run out.

In the area of relationships, you will become dependent on God as the source of your primary relationship. Your attachment to others will be given up in the Wilderness in the physical sense, so that a new opportunity for conscious awareness between the Creator and yourself can now take place. Also, an authentic relationship between you and yourself can now take place as well.

Leaving Egypt at first appears to be exhilarating after the initial goodbye. Your time and your life are now yours. They belong to you. You get to be still and not have to do. You have many ideas about what your journey ahead will look like and what you will do with your newly-found freedom.

I regret having to share this truth with you, especially as this is a precarious part of your journey when you are first leaving Egypt. However, it is necessary to be forewarned - the journey you have decided to undertake is for the spiritual development of your soul, and I would not describe it as being fun or easy. You will be required to do a lot of challenging work of an inner nature that will take all of your strength, and your ability to persevere through seemingly insurmountable obstacles.

This is a trek through harsh inner climates, and through many internal mountains of obstacles and seas of fear. I am not trying to scare you, but I need to paint a realistic picture of what you are agreeing to embark upon when you make a decision to take the journey of the soul. The voyage is not the fantasy that we create in our minds.

Then why embark on it, you may ask. Why leave my safe, comfortable, and prosperous environment to endure the opposite? That is a good question, and one you must be sure of the answer to before you leave Egypt.

The soul that departs Egypt does so because it cannot stay there any longer or it will die in the sense that it will be relegated back to the outer barren reaches of your consciousness once again. The obstacles awaiting the soul on the journey are more preferable to it than the conditions that deny its existence in Egypt. You will be called upon to shed your false human identity as being who you truly are, and to stop identifying with the ego as yourself.

If you can deny your soul's call resounding in you to journey, I suggest that you do so. Leaving Egypt is the beginning of a life of experiences that will change the very essence of who you are.

<u>(Respond to Reflection Question 1)</u>

I ask you this because before long this will become your reality. If you cannot accept this, then do not leave Egypt. You are not yet ready. There is no condemnation for not being ready. Your time has not yet come.

You will not be asked to give up all material things or people all at once. You will have some time to ease into it, but eventually they will have to go. Not because they are wrong in any way, but because a new you is emerging, one that will require you to remove your focus from outer things for at least a while.

(Respond to Reflection Questions 2, 3, and 4)

You will gain back all of things that you were asked to give up in Egypt later on in the journey. However, they will no longer represent to you what they once did. You will gain them back through a spirit-filled consciousness instead of an ego one. All is not lost. Be of good cheer. You can do this! But only if there is no longer any option left for you to do so. It bears repeating: leave Egypt only if you can no longer ignore your soul's call to take this journey.

Some of us did not voluntarily agree to take this journey. These conditions were thrust upon us by force of circumstances, such as losing a job, or being left, or a foreclosure. Regardless of what caused you to leave Egypt, you have a decision to make - will you consciously start the journey that you are on, or will you see yourself as a victim of your circumstances? Which choice you make will determine how your time out of Egypt will be spent.

Will your efforts be spent trying to return to Egypt, or will part of you realize that there are no coincidences in life? You are where you need to be to evolve spiritually. The question is, will you take the journey of the soul consciously, or deny the existence of a spiritual purpose for where you find yourself?

(Respond to Reflection Questions 5 and 6)

There is no such thing as randomness. This suggests that there is no order to the Universe. God did not create you randomly. The circumstances that are challenging you to leave Egypt have not come randomly. They have come to urge you to start the journey of your soul; whether or not you will do so is up to you.

(Respond to Reflection Questions 7 to 9)

REFLECTION QUESTIONS

- Once you leave Egypt, if you become homeless and penniless, lose family and friends, and lose all material prestige in the eyes of the world, who are you? (Q1)

- What are your fears about leaving Egypt? (Q2)

- What are your fears about remaining in Egypt? (Q3)

- Are you voluntarily leaving Egypt? (Q4)

- If you are not leaving Egypt voluntarily, but through force of circumstances, do you believe that your thoughts and feelings about your life over a long period of time held in consciousness played no part in you leaving Egypt? Describe the thoughts and feelings that you have been carrying around in your subconscious which has led to your exodus from Egypt. (Q5)

- Do you believe that the events which occur in your life are random? (Q6)

- Describe any events that occurred in your life that seem divinely ordered (Q7)

- Does any part of you feel restless with your current life? Do you long for a change? How intense is this feeling? (Q8)

- Are you living the life of your dreams? Which areas of your life fall short? (Q9)

REFLECTION ANSWERS

Question # _____

_____
_____
_____
_____
_____
_____

Question # _____

_____
_____
_____
_____
_____
_____
_____

Question # _____

_____
_____
_____
_____
_____
_____

REFLECTION ANSWERS

Question # _____

_____
_____
_____
_____
_____
_____

Question # _____

_____
_____
_____
_____
_____
_____

Question # _____

_____
_____
_____
_____
_____
_____

REFLECTION ANSWERS

Question # _____

_____
_____
_____
_____
_____
_____

Question # _____

_____
_____
_____
_____
_____
_____

Question # _____

_____
_____
_____
_____
_____
_____

REFLECTION ANSWERS

Question # _____

Question # _____

Question # _____

- Make a list of your life goals. Put a star by how many you have already achieved. Determine how many you have yet to achieve. How important to you are the remaining goals?

- Complete a vision page of your ideal life. What would it look like? Use words/and or pictures to help.

- List all of the titles that you have. Then draw a line through all of them (crossing them out). Describe how this makes you feel.

- Choose the ideal age that you wish to retire. Describe what retirement would look and feel like for you.

- State the following aloud: "I am no longer dependent on a paycheck." Then verbally affirm multiple times a day: "God is the source of my supply."

- Mentally picture a scenario where you are surrounded by all of your fulfilled desires. Attune yourself with the energy of how this feels. Reside in this vibrational space often.

Journal

Red Sea

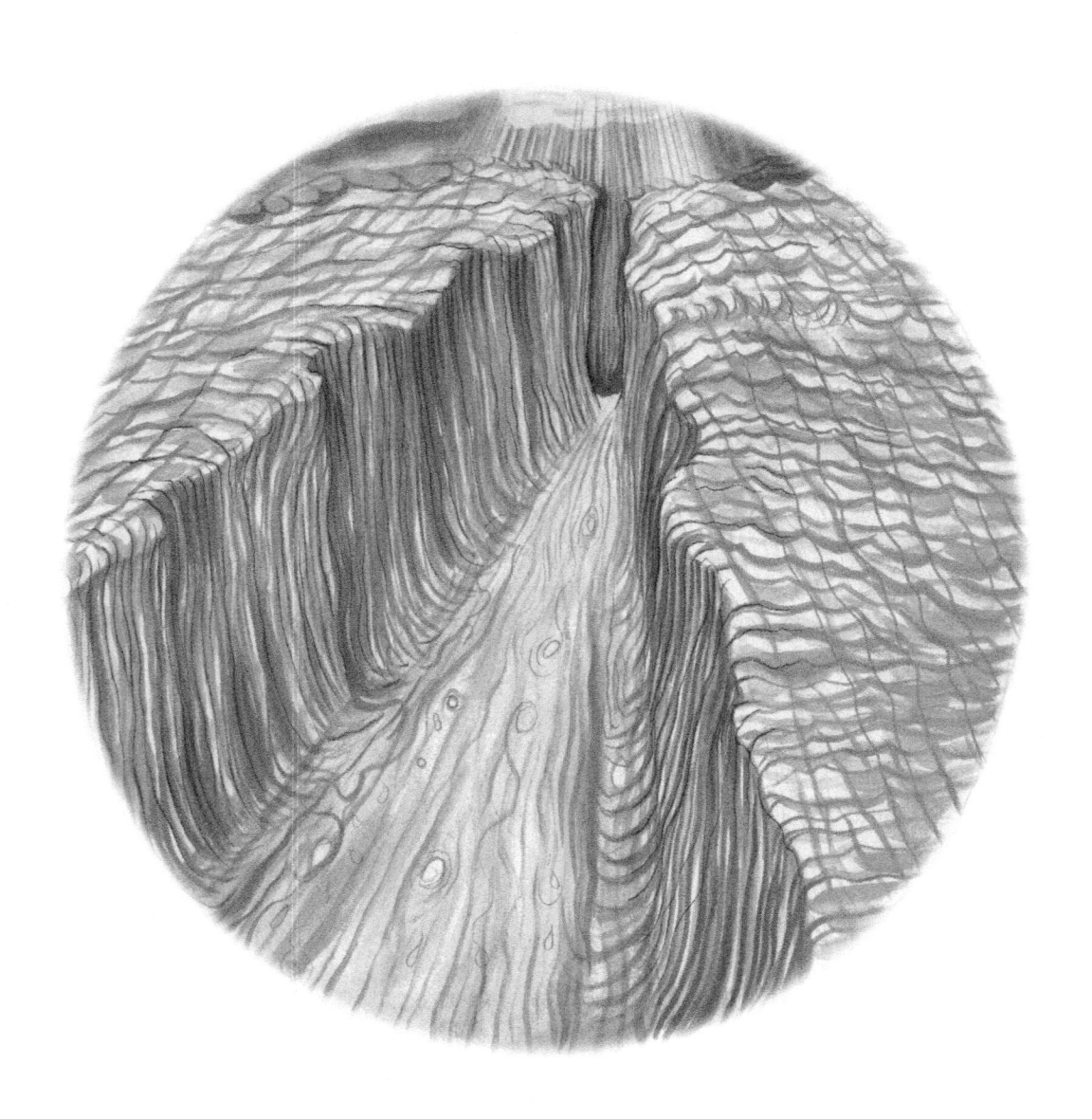

CAN I CROSS OVER THE SEA OF MY FEARS?

Select a number between 1 and 7 (with 7 being the highest) that reflects how true each statement is for you presently.

☐ I am ready to take a leap of faith.

☐ The fear of losing contact with my soul is stronger than my fear of leaving where presently am.

☐ I can no longer force myself to physically show up.

☐ I am disconnecting emotionally from where I am.

☐ I have unwavering faith that a higher power is guiding me.

☐ My faith in God is stronger than my fears.

☐ The time has come to give up my dreams and a higher way of existence forever unless I take some action now.

Add the numbers in all of the boxes together, and shade in the total number in the bar graph below. Revisit this activity periodically to gauge your readiness to cross over the sea of your fears.

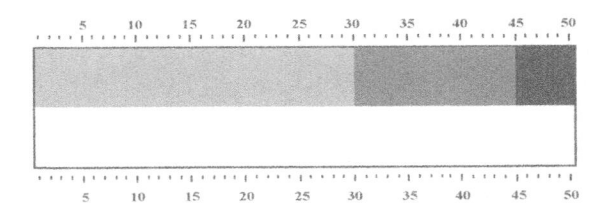

I am in this stage of spiritual development.
I am in the process of evolving.
I am ready to leave this stage of spiritual development.

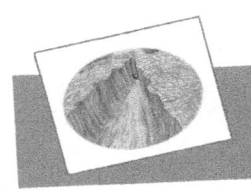

Insight

The Red Sea level of spiritual development is when you decide to take a leap of faith into an unknown future. You cut the ties that hold you in material bondage in Egypt, creating an opening through the center of your fears long enough for you to reach solid land in the Wilderness.

You will look back often to Egypt, but if you look back for too long, and resist moving forward, then you will become surrounded by the seas of your fear again in consciousness, eliminating your entry into the Wilderness.

(Respond to Reflection Questions)

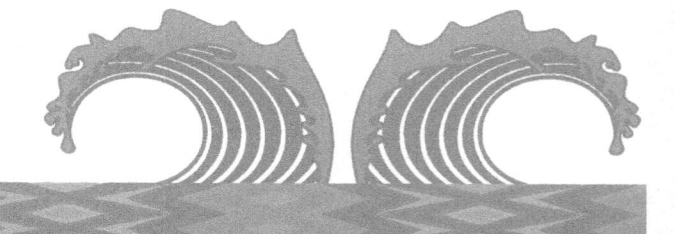

REFLECTION QUESTIONS

- Is your faith strong enough for you to leave Egypt? (Q1)

- Describe the circumstances in which you decided to leave Egypt. (Q2)

- How do people in Egypt seek to keep you in bondage there? (Q3)

- Now that you have left Egypt, describe any emotions that you are feeling (Q4)

- What feelings of guilt over leaving Egypt still linger in your consciousness? (Q5)

- Are you still looking back to what used to be? Are you attached to something in Egypt that you are finding hard to let go? (Q6)

- What are some of the things that tempt you to return to Egypt? (Q7)

REFLECTION ANSWERS

Question # _____

Question # _____

Question # _____

REFLECTION ANSWERS

Question # _____

Question # _____

Question # _____

Reflection Answers

Question # _____

Question # _____

Question # _____

RED SEA ACTIVITIES

- Create a mental scenario where you decide to go back to Egypt and resume your old way of life. Then identify the emotions which arise in you over the notion of returning to Egypt.

- Visualize mentally that a door has closed behind you and that when you try to open it you cannot. Then visualize another door in front of you. Try to open it, and write down or draw what happens.

- Identify times when you feel fear the most. Test out some methods to try and lessen it, such as taking deep breaths.

- Make a clear delineation between the fears you are feeling being separate from your true identity. When you feel fear, recite a litany that you create to alleviate it. Refuse to identify with fear as having authority over you.

- List all the reasons why going back to Egypt will not serve your spiritual development.

- When you are feeling down or depressed, withdraw your attention from your emotions, and connect with the silence found within you either through meditation, a quiet walk, or by doing some spiritual activity that soothes your spirit.

Journal

Wilderness

WHO AM I?

Check off however many of these statements apply to you. If you have checked at least seven of these boxes you are in the Wilderness stage of spiritual development.

- ☐ I am no longer gainfully employed.

- ☐ I am no longer married.

- ☐ I no longer have a title (Mrs., Manager etc.) that defines me.

- ☐ My life is at a standstill.

- ☐ I do not know where my life is headed.

- ☐ Money is going out, but none is coming in.

- ☐ I have lost my material possessions.

- ☐ I no longer have my own place to live.

- ☐ I am lost.

- ☐ I am terrified.

Insight

The Wilderness is the place where you truly get to know God for the first time. It is also the place where you come into contact with an alienated part of yourself—your spirit.

<u>(Respond to Reflection Questions 1-16)</u>

These are some of the questions that you must answer in the Wilderness stage of spiritual development before you can leave it. So I ask you again: who are you now that you have been stripped of your human identity? If you do not know, it is time to find out. You must excavate the lost parts of yourself.

When you were a child, what brought you joy (reading, painting, singing, dancing, etc.)? Whatever it was, start doing it again now. Draw a picture, sing aloud. Why? You must get back in touch with expressing simple joy in being. In fact, find one thing that brings you joy and do it once a day. It does not matter what it is, but you must do this exercise to get you back in touch with feeling simple joy (build houses with Lego blocks, color in a coloring book, etc.).

Write down your fears regularly. If you can state them, they will eventually lose the power that they have over you. Maybe not the first few times, or the hundredth, but eventually they will leave. Write them down and then cease thinking about them. Once they are on paper, release them to God. Do this whenever fear arises in you. Say, "I release you to God." Fear and God cannot exist in the same mental space. You can focus on one or the other, but not both at the same time.

Choose to place your focus on God, and fear will dissipate in the moment. However, it will soon return. You have to be diligent in combating it by choosing to focus on God, which can take many forms such as meditating, reading spiritual books, listening to uplifting music, and praying.

Although you may not want to hear this, everything that you greatly fear will come to pass in the Wilderness. There is no way to avoid this. This is why people leave the Wilderness before the appointed time. It proves to be too hard for most. The Wilderness is the place where you are called upon to battle you fears by facing them firsthand. Experiencing your fears will not destroy you, but avoidance of them may.

Where is God?

You cannot feel his/her presence. You can no longer hear his voice. This is because when you are in the grips of fear, you vibrate at such a low level that you cannot reach God. God cannot reach you either, because you have tuned him out. Remember, fear and God cannot reside in the same place mentally. You must give one up for the other. Can you shut fear down for, say, an hour a day, so that you can be in mental silence? Here you will find God.

Negotiate with yourself. I will give in to fear for the rest of the day, but for this hour I will take a reprieve. Gradually increase the amount of hours you surrender fear until you are experiencing fear for only an hour or less a day.

The only way to take control of your mind is to vibrate at a higher level than fear and worry. You must fill your inner storehouse with so much positive energy that you reside on a higher level than fear resides on. However, these are only temporary fixes. The only way to defeat your fears once and for all is to experience them actualizing.

(Respond to Reflection Questions 17 and 18)

Are you still alive?

Yes, you are! Fear did not kill you. Fear is energy that seeks to keep you stuck. While in the midst of fear, you must move through it. Realize this when you are facing your fears.

Call on God. Do whatever it takes: cry, beseech, demand, plead and make promises. Realize that you are not doing this for the sake of God. You are the one who needs reassurance that God really hears you. In truth, God is always with you.

After reaching out to God, something starts to awaken in you: a self that is detached from what is happening externally in your life. You will start to make contact with a newly-awakened part of you. If you can keep in contact with this part of you during the challenges that you are experiencing in your life, it will make things easier. This part of you, your spirit, serves as your lifeline. Cling diligently to it.

<u>(Respond to Reflection Questions 19-21)</u>

The truth is, when you give up your will and refuse to take it back, you will find yourself strangely at peace. Yes, the fear is still there, but so is peace. The peace stems from the realization that you are no longer alone. If you allow God to be in charge of all of your life, your life will change for the better.

A dependent being is a being that depends on God for everything: food, clothing, shelter, money, work, relationships, health and life itself. When your relationship with God develops, you and the Creator become partners in creation. Allow God to act through you. Your job is to empty yourself of you—your ego and all its desires.

In this place of emptiness, God will fill you. You are no longer entitled to your will. You may think that God's will may not be the same as your will. You are correct: it's not. The ego's will can never be the same as God's. However, God's will authentically represents the will of your higher self.
Your spirit came to Earth with an agenda, and you replaced it with your own ego agenda. The unhappiness, despair, restlessness and pain you feel is coming from your soul that is dying inside of you, and is making a last-ditch effort to reach you before it's too late.

Now that you have come this far, it is time to let your Moses consciousness go. Moses has led you as far as he can. He took you out of Egypt, through the Red Sea, and wandered with you in the Wilderness. It is time for Joshua to become the supreme ruler of your thoughts, and to lead you through the Jordan River to the Promised Land. In order for Joshua to be born within you, you must now align yourself with your spirit as being your true and only identity. Your spirit has one prevailing desire. It asks, "How can I serve?" The ego asks, "How can I serve myself?" The spirit in its wisdom knows that the highest way that you can serve yourself is through service to God.

It is now time for you to become a servant. Do not attempt to figure out in what capacity you will serve. The Source of all already knows in which capacity you will serve. Allow it be revealed to you. You may balk at what you are being asked to do, because it does not match the ego's desire for prestige or recognition. God knows what is in your heart. He placed authentic desires there in the first place. Your desires of the heart were to serve as a beacon signal from your spirit to lead you on the right path.

You must realize that we are on a journey, a journey where we go through many stages of spiritual development. When you identify yourself as being spirit, when you are ready to serve, and when the I Am has shown you in what capacity you are to serve, your Wilderness experience is over. Where you are now in consciousness requires you to start at a beginning level in work of a service nature. Realize that you may need further experience or education in order to become fully prepared to do what is being asked of you.

It is now time to re-enter the outer world. Notice that I did no say real world, because nothing will ever be more real to you than the time you have just spent with God in the Wilderness. The closeness and dependency on God that emerged during this stage of development will serve you for the rest of your life.

Remember that you are now a dependent being. God will bring about the opportunities for you to serve. Your job is to recognize them when they are sent, and to take immediate action. Things that you deem as coincidences will point you in the direction of where you are to serve.

Do not balk at the low pay that you will be offered, or at not having a lofty title. Where you are at now is only a stepping stone leading you to the Promised Land. In fact, you will be so happy to leave the Wilderness that you will be glad to accept any position to serve.

(Respond to Reflection Questions 22-28)

REFLECTION QUESTIONS

⚜ Which part of you do you authentically identify with in the Wilderness: your ego or your spirit? (Q1)

⚜ Recall the reasons why you decided to leave Egypt. (Q2)

⚜ What, if any, regrets do you have over your decision to leave Egypt? (Q3)

⚜ In this place where you seemingly lost it all, do you feel like a failure? (Q4)

⚜ Once you give up your material identity, can you identify with a nonmaterial part of you that feels alive for the first time? (Q5)

⚜ How long have you been in the Wilderness? Does it seem even longer than the actual time you have spent here? (Q6)

⚜ Do you feel abandonment by God? (Q7)

⚜ Do you pray? If so, what do you pray for? (Q8)

⚜ Describe any feelings of boredom and loneliness in the Wilderness. (Q9)

⚜ Have you lost any friends, family, or relationships? (Q10)

⚜ How do you spend your days in the Wilderness? (Q11)

⚜ Does any part of you feel as though it's dying? Which aspect is dying, and why? (Q12)

⚜ List your current frustrations. (Q13)

⚜ How are you resisting your current spiritual stage of development? (Q14)

⚜ What are you seeking to accomplish through your own efforts? (Q15)

REFLECTION QUESTIONS

🌿 Once you stop resisting being in the Wilderness, do you feel depressed? (Q16)

🌿 What are some techniques you can utilize to quiet your mind, in order to refrain from negative thinking? (Q17)

🌿 How will you feel after your fears have actualized into physical reality? (Q18)

🌿 What are your fears about permanently surrendering your will to God? (Q19)

🌿 After you surrender your will, describe any part of you that now feels relieved and unburdened. (Q20)

🌿 In what ways have you been provided for, after surrendering your will and becoming totally dependent on God for your sustenance? (Q21)

🌿 List the illusions that you still cling to which need to be given up. (Q22)

🌿 How can you reevaluate the purpose of romantic relationships from a spiritual perspective? (Q23)

🌿 Do you believe in miracles? (Q24)

🌿 List all of the things that you deem as miracles that occurred in the Wilderness. (Q25)

🌿 What is it that you most desire to manifest? (Q26)

🌿 How has God asked you to be of service in the world? (Q27)

🌿 What are your feelings about the type of service that you have been led to do? (Q28)

REFLECTION ANSWERS

Question # _____

_____
_____
_____
_____
_____

Question # _____

_____
_____
_____
_____
_____

Question # _____

_____
_____
_____
_____
_____

REFLECTION ANSWERS

Question # _____

_____

_____

_____

_____

_____

_____

Question # _____

_____

_____

_____

_____

_____

_____

Question # _____

_____

_____

_____

_____

_____

_____

REFLECTION ANSWERS

Question # _____

_____
_____
_____
_____
_____

Question # _____

_____
_____
_____
_____
_____

Question # _____

_____
_____
_____
_____
_____

REFLECTION ANSWERS

Question # _____

_____
_____
_____
_____
_____
_____
_____

Question # _____

_____
_____
_____
_____
_____
_____
_____
_____

Question # _____

_____
_____
_____
_____
_____
_____
_____

Reflection Answers

REFLECTION ANSWERS

Question # _____

_____
_____
_____
_____
_____
_____
_____

Question # _____

_____
_____
_____
_____
_____
_____
_____

Question # _____

_____
_____
_____
_____
_____
_____

Reflection Answers

Question # _____

Question # _____

Question # _____

Reflection Answers

Question # _____

_____
_____
_____
_____
_____
_____
_____

Question # _____

_____
_____
_____
_____
_____
_____
_____
_____

Question # _____

_____
_____
_____
_____
_____
_____
_____

REFLECTION ANSWERS

Question # _____

_____
_____
_____
_____
_____
_____
_____

Question # _____

_____
_____
_____
_____
_____
_____
_____
_____

Question # _____

_____
_____
_____
_____
_____
_____
_____

REFLECTION ANSWERS

Question # _____

_____
_____
_____
_____
_____
_____

Question # _____

_____
_____
_____
_____
_____
_____

Question # _____

_____
_____
_____
_____
_____
_____

REFLECTION ANSWERS

Question # _____

_____
_____
_____
_____
_____
_____

Question # _____

_____
_____
_____
_____
_____
_____

Question # _____

_____
_____
_____
_____
_____
_____

REFLECTION ANSWERS

Question # _____

Question # _____

Question # _____

Reflection Answers

Question # _____

_____
_____
_____
_____
_____
_____

Question # _____

_____
_____
_____
_____
_____
_____
_____

Question # _____

_____
_____
_____
_____
_____
_____

WILDERNESS ACTIVITIES

- Contact acquaintances and share your journey with those who are sympathetic to your struggles. Acquaintances will be the very people whom God sends to help you in your time of need; more than your closest friends and family.

- Make a conscious decision to live for each day in the Wilderness, with no thought about tomorrow. Try not to deviate from this plan.

- Create a consciousness of flexibility. The Wilderness will cause you to wander from place to place, and if you resist your diminished level of materiality, you will find evolving more painful than it needs to be. Approach your wandering with the mindset of a grand adventure that you are on. If you choose to take the approach that you are on an adventure, your perception about what is occurring in your life will change.

- Take an inventory of all of your material items and release the nonessential ones. Be prepared to move at a moment's notice with your essential items.

- Find peaceful activities to relax you; and do at least one a day. Complete the following sentence: What relaxes me the most is ...

- Color in the mandalas in this section as an exercise in mindfulness and relaxation.

- Surrender your will daily to a higher power. Create an affirmation of surrender and repeat it as needed.

- The most important activity that you can do in the Wilderness is to cultivate the presence of inner silence. This creates an open channel between you and God, allowing a conversation to begin.

Journal

Jordan River

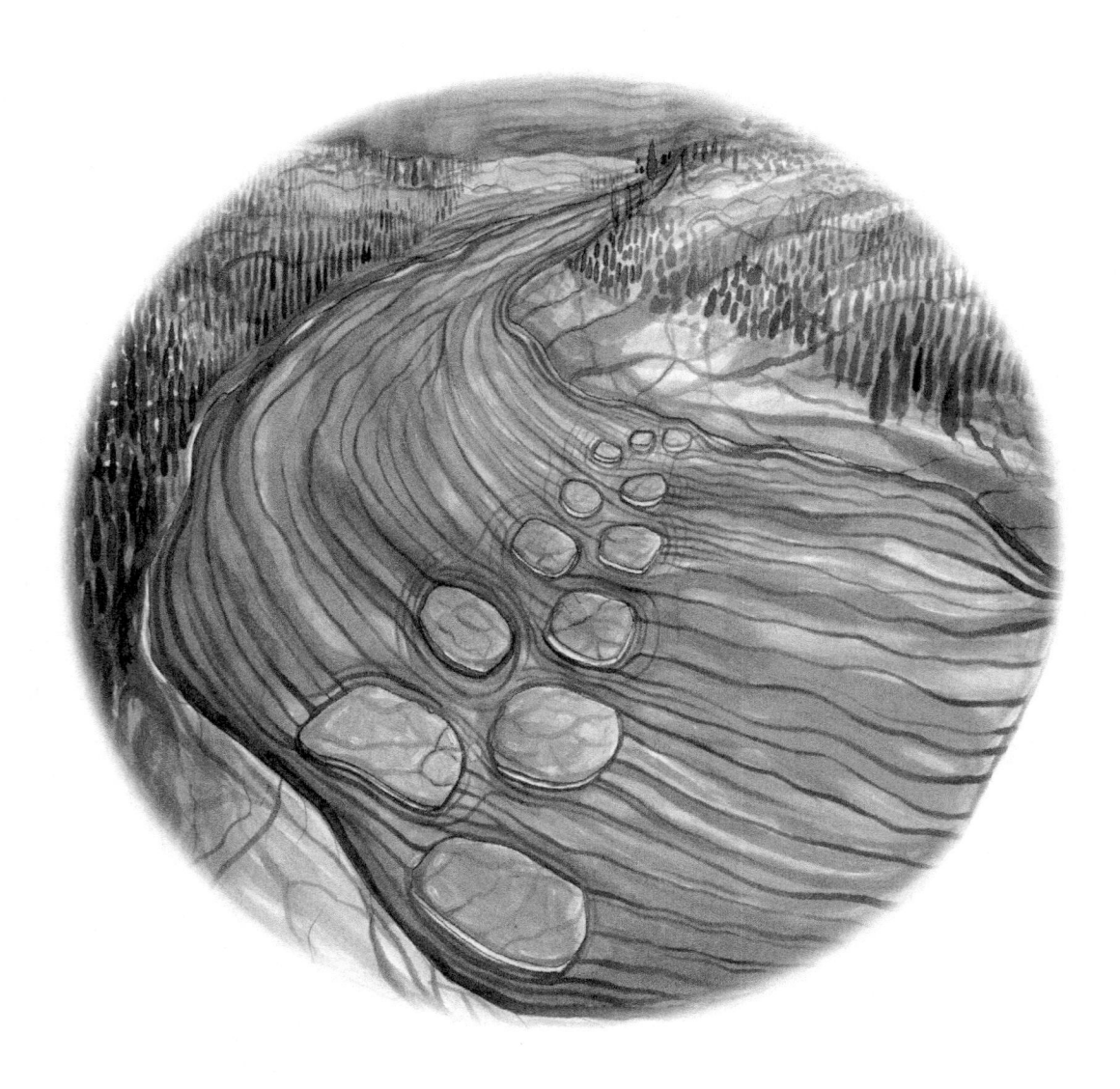

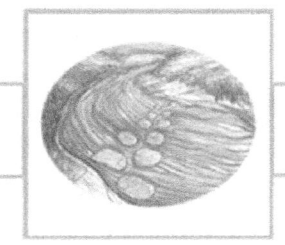

AM I READY TO ENTER THE JORDAN RIVER?

Select a number between 1 and 7 (with 7 being the highest) that reflects how true each statement is for you presently.

- ☐ I know I am a spiritual being having a human experience.

- ☐ I long to serve in some capacity.

- ☐ I have completely surrendered my will to God.

- ☐ I am totally dependent on God for everything.

- ☐ I have no ego desires separate from God.

- ☐ I feel closer to God now than I ever have.

- ☐ I have been led to take an entry level service job.

- ☐ I no longer feel burdened, and feel like the weight of the world is off my shoulders.

- ☐ I believe in miracles.

- ☐ I am at peace.

Add the numbers in all of the boxes together, and shade in the total number in the bar graph below. Revisit this activity periodically to gauge your readiness to leave the Jordan River stage of spiritual development.

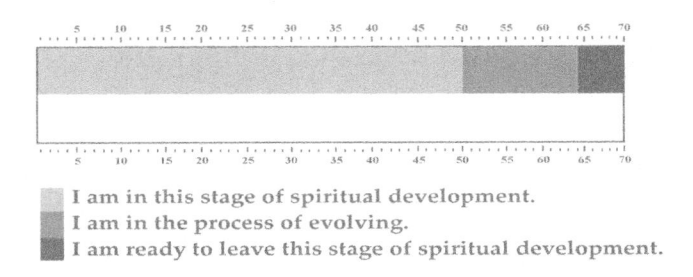

I am in this stage of spiritual development.
I am in the process of evolving.
I am ready to leave this stage of spiritual development.

Insight

You will also witness many miracles in the Jordan River. Although you have been led by spirit to move to higher ground, and to expand your territory in consciousness, the ego mind is still your adversary. You must learn to overcome it in order to be able to fully manifest the desires of your heart. If you still identify with the ego mind and in the manner in which it thinks, your manifestations will be delayed indefinitely.

You must overcome your fears in the Jordan River and cross over them in consciousness. The only way to do this is to face them head-on. Your fears differ from the ones you faced in the Wilderness. You have to overcome your fears about receiving your good.

(Respond to Reflection Questions 1 and 2)

Although a part of you believes in miracles, your ego mind, which you still are partially attached to, requires proof. So you are in a quandary; you must proceed in faith without proof. This is your first test when you enter the Jordan River for the first time. Will the waters part for you to cross over your fears?

Yes, they will. However, you must step one by one over the remaining barriers or stones that are weighing you down in consciousness. Remember, fear keeps you stuck, so you must keep on moving in the Jordan River and not linger for too long.

God will send even more clues about your ultimate destination when you are in the Jordan River phrase of spiritual development. You will not remain here as long as you did in the Wilderness. Your time spent here can range up to two years.

You will not feel at home in the Jordan River, or that you belong in this land. This is because it is a stepping stone to propel you in consciousness to where you are going next. It is not a stage where you settle down. You will be in the outer world, but you will not truly feel part of it.

(Respond to Reflection Questions 3 and 4)

You will feel alienated from those around you. This is because you know that the pursuits found in the outer world are not real. Your spirit refuses to reengage belief in false illusions. The people around you may not understand why you separate yourself from them. You will feel acutely alone here. There are few people that will understand you.

You separate yourself from others through your actions because your spirit knows that you are heading somewhere else. This is merely a pit stop for you, whereas it may be the final destination for others. You are not like everyone else in this land. You are a visitor, with your final destination being the Promised Land.

You are on the journey of the soul. They are on a path of the ego's making and choosing. Do not condemn them, but you must be aware of the difference between where they are and where you are, or you will see yourself as lacking in some way. Do not fall into this trap while in the Jordan River. You lack nothing of any true value.

The material is no longer the master that we serve, nor is the ego and its insane belief system. You will not seek to compete at work or school, be like others in romantic relationships, or seek to fit in and act like others in the Jordan River. You will not accept the ego rewards that you may be offered here, although you may often be tempted. You have been awoken to the truth, and you cannot go back to sleep. Your promise of fulfillment lies elsewhere. This is what separates you: now you can only find fulfillment in spiritual pursuits and endeavors.

(Respond to Reflection Questions 5, 6, 7 and 8)

Here is where we lose many people. Will the God that led you out of Egypt, parted the Red Sea of your fears, and provided for you in the Wilderness abandon you now? This is a question that you must answer for yourself before you can proceed. Despite how much you enjoyed your Jordan River experience, it is time to leave it. This is no time for complacency, but a time to be bold and of courage.

What is the worst that can happen? You survived the journey thus far. It is time to take another leap of faith. Know that just like at the entrance of the Red Sea, God will part the Jordan River for you, and he will take you to the shores of the long-awaited Promised Land.

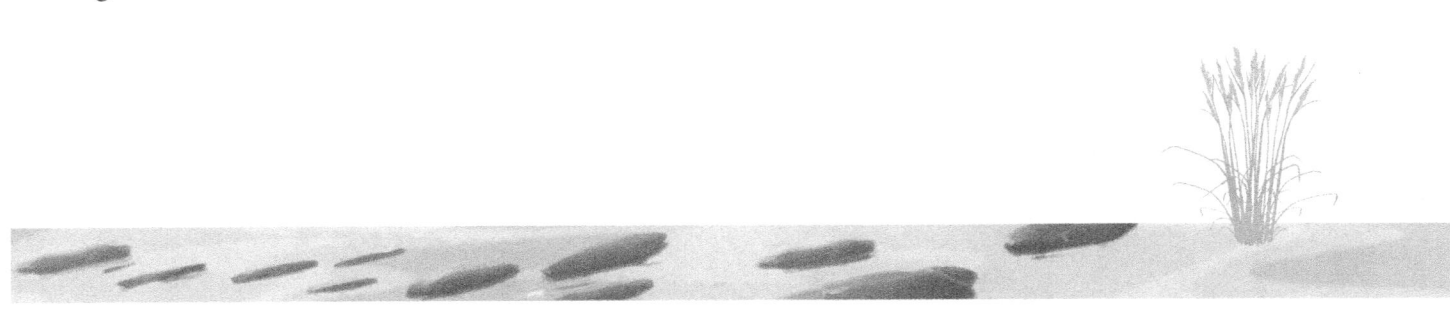

However, before you can enter it, you must surrender your will and even your heart's desire one last time. We become so attached to our dream that we start to place it on an altar and worship it. The dream was given to you by God. Worship God! Love the dream, but release it now. This is your final test. Can you give up what you have so diligently sought? The reason for this test is to ascertain whom you serve? Do you serve your spirit, or your ego who has turned your dream into its property—disguised as the will of God?

If you cannot give up your dream now, then you are not coming from a place of spirit. You have allowed the ego to sneak in, and make you attached once more to its dictates. Attachment, even to spiritual things, must be released. You do not pursue spiritual pursuits for ego glory, but for the glory of God whom you serve.

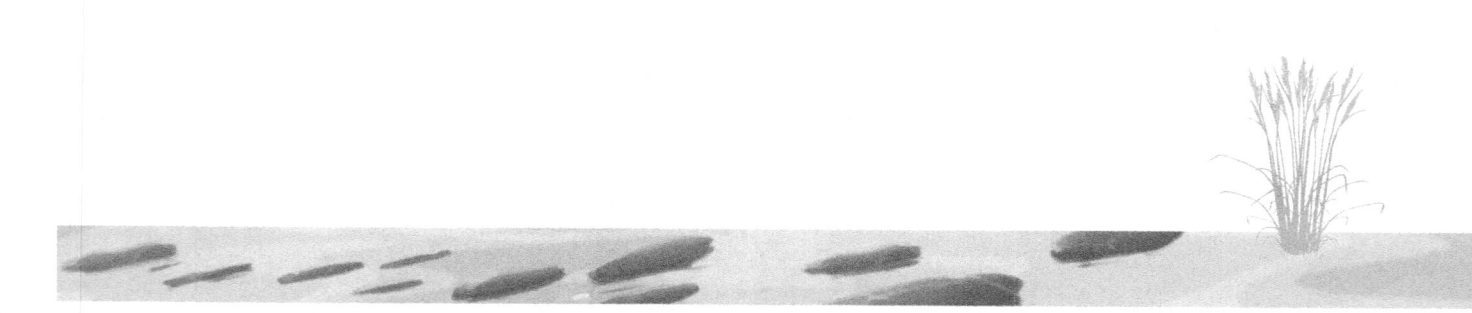

REFLECTION QUESTIONS

🜂 What are your spiritual gifts? (Q1)

🜂 What is your divine purpose in life? (Q2)

🜂 List the remaining obstacles to you accomplishing your heart's desires? (Q3)

🜂 How can you formulate a spiritual plan of action for overcoming these obstacles? (Q4)

🜂 Name any remaining fears which arise within you when it is time to leave the Jordan River. (Q5)

🜂 How can you prevent these fears from keeping you from crossing the Jordan River and entering the Promised Land? (Q6)

🜂 What is your vision of your Promised Land? (Q7)

🜂 What is your connection like to God, the Creator, or a Higher Power? (Q8)

🜂 Are you willing to release your dream back to God, and walk away from it? (Q9)

REFLECTION ANSWERS

Question # _____

Question # _____

Question # _____

REFLECTION ANSWERS

Question # _____

_____
_____
_____
_____
_____
_____

Question # _____

_____
_____
_____
_____
_____
_____

Question # _____

_____
_____
_____
_____
_____

REFLECTION ANSWERS

Question # _____

Question # _____

Question # _____

REFLECTION ANSWERS

Question # _____

_____
_____
_____
_____
_____
_____

Question # _____

_____
_____
_____
_____
_____
_____
_____
_____

Question # _____

_____
_____
_____
_____
_____
_____
_____

JORDAN RIVER ACTIVITIES

- Divine Escrow Activity: Fill in your name on the checks provided for you in this section. This helps you to align in vibrational frequency to the feeling of abundance.

- Use the blank checks in this section to fill in an amount of money needed to pay off your largest debts. This allows you to see the debts paid in full, before it occurs in physical reality. This sets a clear intention for debt relief.

- Keep a log of the major milestones that you reach in the Jordan River.

- Assign a time to regularly connect with spirit daily despite your busy schedule.

- Maintain a spirit of gratitude in spite of the challenges that this stage offers.

- Use the appreciation pages to make a list of the things that you appreciate in your life.

- Create a mental scenario to aid you when problems arise that sap your strength. This is a mental exercise to deny the power of physical reality over you. One example is to visualize yourself as being Daniel in the lions' den. Imagine the lions at your back, ready to devour you, but you keep your back turned to them. Instead, look up to the east, waiting in faith for deliverance from God. Draw or post a photo of your scenario up at home.

Escrow Account

PAY TO THE ORDER OF _____ 20____ DATE

$ 100.00

One Hundred and Zero Cents _____ DOLLARS

Bank of Divine Compensation

For: Right of Consciousness

Divine Creator

PAY TO THE ORDER OF _____ 20____ DATE

$ 1000.00

One Thousand and Zero Cents _____ DOLLARS

Bank of Divine Compensation

For: Right of Consciousness

Divine Creator

PAY TO THE ORDER OF _____ 20____ DATE

$ 10,000.00

Ten Thousand and Zero Cents _____ DOLLARS

Bank of Divine Compensation

For: Right of Consciousness

Divine Creator

PAY TO THE ORDER OF _____ 20____ DATE

$ 100,000.00

One Hundred Thousand and Zero Cents _____ DOLLARS

Bank of Divine Compensation

For: Right of Consciousness

Divine Creator

PAY TO THE ORDER OF _____ 20____ DATE

$ 1,000,000.00

One Million _____ DOLLARS

Bank of Divine Compensation

For: Right of Consciousness

Divine Creator

Escrow Account

PAY TO THE
ORDER OF _____

20____ DATE

$ _____

_____ DOLLARS

Bank of Divine Compensation

For: Right of Consciousness _____

Divine Creator

PAY TO THE
ORDER OF _____

20____ DATE

$ _____

_____ DOLLARS

Bank of Divine Compensation

For: Right of Consciousness _____

Divine Creator

PAY TO THE
ORDER OF _____

20____ DATE

$ _____

_____ DOLLARS

Bank of Divine Compensation

For: Right of Consciousness _____

Divine Creator

PAY TO THE
ORDER OF _____

20____ DATE

$ _____

_____ DOLLARS

Bank of Divine Compensation

For: Right of Consciousness _____

Divine Creator

PAY TO THE
ORDER OF _____

20____ DATE

$ _____

_____ DOLLARS

Bank of Divine Compensation

For: Right of Consciousness _____

Divine Creator

Journal

Promised Land

 **AM I READY TO ENTER THE PROMISE LAND?**

Check off however many of these statements apply to you. If you have checked off all of these boxes then you are ready to enter into The Promised Land.

☐ God/Source told me it was time to leave the Jordan River.

☐ Despite my fears I am willing to leave the Jordan River now without delay.

☐ I have a sufficient amount of faith left in God to lead me to The Promised Land.

☐ I am not willing to settle for the ego's version of The Promised Land.

☐ I will not allow the ego to seduce me with material titles, money, or complacency.

☐ I am eager to enter The Promised Land.

☐ I want to see the journey through to completion.

☐ I will never truly be happy or satisfied with anything less than my Promised Land.

☐ By right of consciousness, I am ready to enter The Promised Land.

Insight

We have arrived on the shores of the Promised Land. Where are the party streamers and horns announcing our joyful arrival? There are none outwardly. However, inwardly you are in a state of pure joy and bliss. You have arrived. Allow this peace to sustain you because when you enter the Promised Land in any life area for the first time, you will have to engage in battle immediately. There are interlopers in the Promised Land that you must overthrow.

After all of my hard work I am being asked to fight yet again? You must conquer your lingering fears that have held the reins of leadership, in order to truly liberate this new land for your own good.

When you enter the Promised Land you will be met with those who seek to challenge your right to be here. You can spend your time focusing on them, or you can see them for what they are—your remaining fears manifesting in physical form in order to provide you with the opportunity to defeat them completely.

Do not focus on what others in this land are telling you. Instead, focus on what to do in order to heal the fears inside of you that are drawing to you these outer attacks.

(Respond to Reflection Questions 1 and 2)

No, the opinions of others about you are not right. However, you fear that they are right. Our criticizers are playing a role, albeit unknowingly. They are being used by spirit to defeat our lingering doubts and fears about our self-worth.

Do not look to others to define who you are. Instead, claim your greatness. This is what you need to do to stop "playing small" and to know that you are great. Then it does not matter who attacks you. It will no longer have any effect on you, and your attackers or teachers will fade into the background.

(Respond to Reflection Questions 3, 4 and 5)

These are some of the thought systems that you must challenge and victoriously overcome. Not doing so will prevent you from progressing far into this new land. You must be a spiritual warrior. When you are attacked, first focus on doing the work in your own consciousness to heal yourself, and then refuse to be affected by the opinions of others.

After you have conquered your foes or fear-filled thoughts, you settle into this new land and begin your work.

(Respond to Reflection Questions 6, 7 and 8)

We must remember that the Promised Land is not about the fulfillment of our ego's desires. It is about the fulfillment of our spirit's desire to be of service. There is only one question to ask in the Promised Land: how can I serve my spirit?

The individual ways in which you serve your spirit in the Promised Land are unique to you. What is important is that you now have the opportunity to do so, which is what God promised you.

You will eventually become restless in your Promised Land. Typically, after seven years of service, you start to dream of leaving it again when you realize that you are no longer serving any of your own individual spiritual needs, just solely the needs of others. Also, when the work that you are doing starts to feel routine, and you become disinterested, then the Promised Land has become Egypt, and it is time for you to leave it.

You will initiate the journey of the soul again from the beginning, with you eventually being led to the second sublevel (of 31 sublevels) of the Promised Land. You did not think that your journey was over, did you?

(Respond to Reflection Question 9)

Reflection Questions

- What adverse thoughts about yourself do you still hold in your subconscious? Are you aware that they are causing others to unconsciously reflect them back to you in the Promised Land? (Q1)

- Why do you still feel unworthy to receive the rewards of your laborious journey? (Q2)

- Do you believe that the opinions of other people: all, some, or none are right about you? (Q3)

- Why are you still playing at being small, and resisting owning up to the greatness that exists inside of you? (Q4)

- State your fears about claiming your greatness. (Q5)

- How can you access the authentic power given to you by your spirit? (Q6)

- Describe the challenges you are facing in the Promised Land. (Q7)

- How can you formulate a spiritual plan of action to overcome these challenges? (Q8)

- Is your spirit urging you to leave the Promised Land? Will you heed its call to journey once again? (Q9)

REFLECTION ANSWERS

Question # _____

_____
_____
_____
_____
_____
_____

Question # _____

_____
_____
_____
_____
_____
_____

Question # _____

_____
_____
_____
_____
_____
_____

REFLECTION ANSWERS

Question # _____

_____
_____
_____
_____
_____
_____

Question # _____

_____
_____
_____
_____
_____
_____

Question # _____

_____
_____
_____
_____
_____
_____

REFLECTION ANSWERS

Question # _____

_____
_____
_____
_____
_____
_____
_____

Question # _____

_____
_____
_____
_____
_____
_____
_____
_____
_____

Question # _____

_____
_____
_____
_____
_____
_____
_____

Reflection Answers

Question # _____

Question # _____

Question # _____

- Take a few moments to bask in feelings of joy when you reach your Promised Land. You have earned it!

- Now prepare yourself for battle, and come up with a battle plan ahead of time to follow when your inner fears over your worth draw outer attacks from others.

- Take an inventory of the remaining fears in your subconscious about your worth. How are you planning to overcome and overthrow these thoughts that hold the reins of leadership?

- See others as a mirror reflecting back your unconscious fears. Do not perceive them as adversaries, but rather as teachers providing necessary lessons for you to learn in order to evolve. Every time someone attacks you in this land ask yourself: How does this person serve as a mirror to my thoughts about me in need of change?

- Dream even bigger dreams. Create a list of increased dreams for you to accomplish; a new Promised Land with increased territory.

- Tend to your own well-being while in the midst of service to others. Plan how you will find balance spiritually between "being" and "doing" while in the Promised Land. Follow this plan once it has been determined.

Journal

Christ Consciousness

I HAVE COMPLETED 31 SUBLEVELS IN THE PROMISED LAND IN ALL AREAS OF MY LIFE.

Check off however many of these statements wholly apply to you. When you have checked off all of these boxes, you have reached the Christ Consciousness stage of spiritual development. This is where our journey together concludes.

☐ I can manifest into physical reality anything that I desire instantaneously.

☐ I no longer come from a place of ego.

☐ God/Source and I are one.

☐ I can commune with higher planes of existence.

☐ I can leave my physical body at will.

☐ The Earth no longer holds any attraction for me.

☐ I see human relationships from a spiritual perspective instead of an ego perspective.

☐ My work on the Earth plane of existence is done.

Resources

Appreciation

......../......./........
I appreciate…

......../......./........
I appreciate…

......../......./........
I appreciate…

......../......./........
I appreciate…

......../......./........
I appreciate…

......../......./........
I appreciate…

......../......./........
I appreciate…

......../......./........
I appreciate…

......../......./........
I appreciate…

......../......./........
I appreciate…

Appreciation

_____ / / _____

I appreciate…

_____
_____
_____
_____
_____
_____
_____

_____ / / _____

I appreciate…

_____
_____
_____
_____
_____
_____
_____

_____ / / _____

I appreciate…

_____
_____
_____
_____
_____
_____
_____

_____ / / _____

I appreciate…

_____
_____
_____
_____
_____
_____
_____

_____ / / _____

I appreciate…

_____
_____
_____
_____
_____
_____
_____

_____ / / _____

I appreciate…

_____
_____
_____
_____
_____
_____

_____ / / _____

I appreciate…

_____
_____
_____
_____
_____
_____

_____ / / _____

I appreciate…

_____
_____
_____
_____
_____
_____

_____ / / _____

I appreciate…

_____
_____
_____
_____
_____
_____

_____ / / _____

I appreciate…

_____
_____
_____
_____
_____
_____

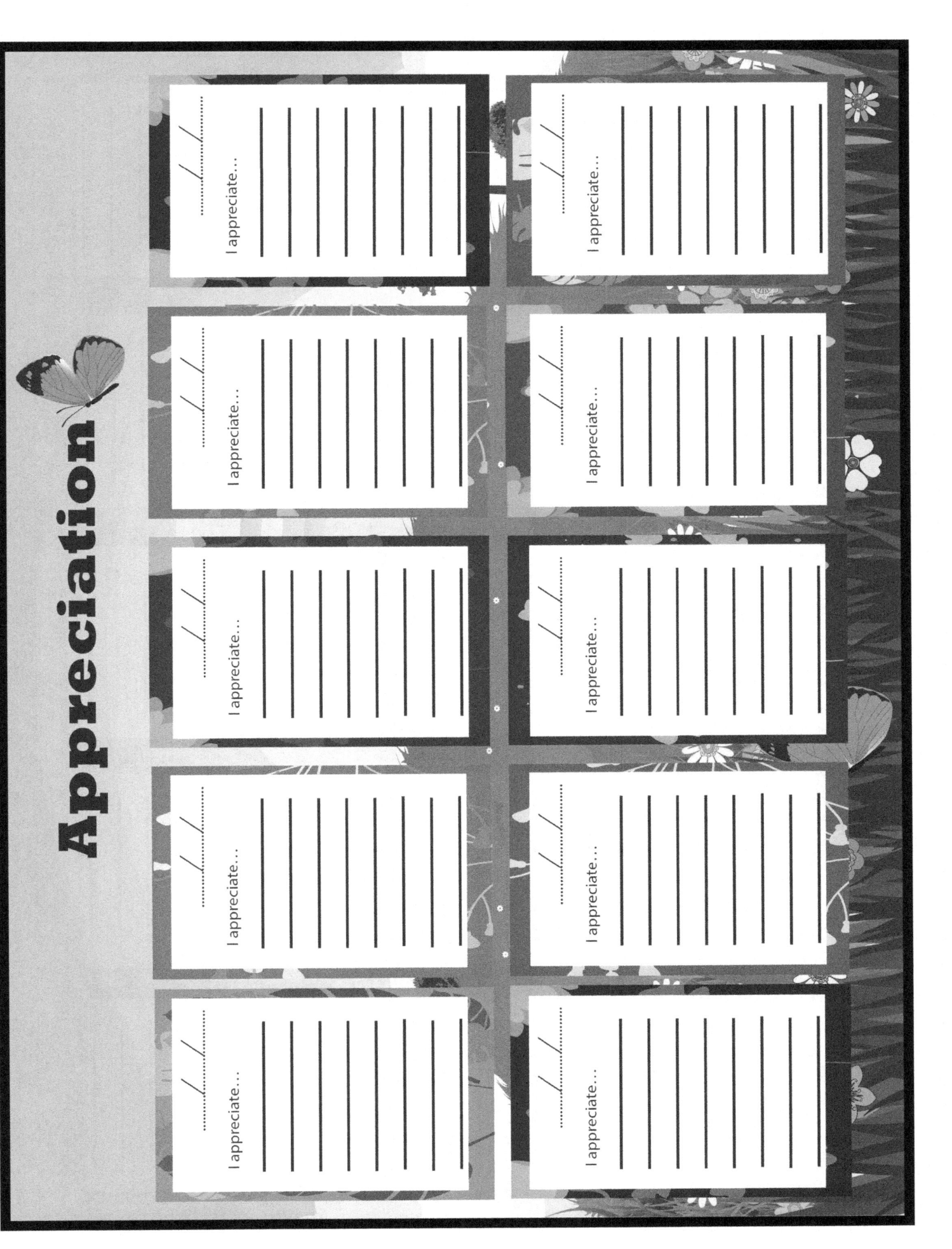

Appreciation

Appreciation

......../......./.......	......../......./.......	......../......./.......	......../......./.......	......../......./.......
I appreciate…	I appreciate…	I appreciate…	I appreciate…	I appreciate…

......../......./.......	......../......./.......	......../......./.......	......../......./.......	......../......./.......
I appreciate…	I appreciate…	I appreciate…	I appreciate…	I appreciate…

Appreciation

............../......./..............	.............../......./..............	.............../......./..............	.............../......./..............	............../......./..............
I appreciate…	I appreciate…	I appreciate…	I appreciate…	I appreciate…

............../......./..............	.............../......./..............	.............../......./..............	.............../......./..............	............../......./..............
I appreciate…	I appreciate…	I appreciate…	I appreciate…	I appreciate…

Appreciation

.........../........../..........
I appreciate…

.........../........../..........
I appreciate…

.........../........../..........
I appreciate…

.........../........../..........
I appreciate…

.........../........../..........
I appreciate…

.........../........../..........
I appreciate…

.........../........../..........
I appreciate…

.........../........../..........
I appreciate…

.........../........../..........
I appreciate…

.........../........../..........
I appreciate…

Monday

/ /

Tuesday

/ /

Wednesday

/ /

Thursday

/ /

Friday

/ /

Saturday

/ /

Sunday

/ /

Notes

/ / **Thursday**	**Notes**
/ / **Wednesday**	/ / **Sunday**
/ / **Tuesday**	/ / **Saturday**
/ / **Monday**	/ / **Friday**

Monday

_____
_____
_____
_____
_____
_____
_____
_____

Tuesday

_____
_____
_____
_____
_____
_____
_____
_____

Wednesday

_____
_____
_____
_____
_____
_____
_____
_____

Thursday

_____
_____
_____
_____
_____
_____
_____
_____

Friday

_____
_____
_____
_____
_____
_____
_____
_____

Saturday

_____
_____
_____
_____
_____
_____
_____
_____

Sunday

_____
_____
_____
_____
_____
_____
_____
_____

Notes

_____
_____
_____
_____
_____
_____
_____
_____

Monday

_____ / _____ / _____

Tuesday

_____ / _____ / _____

Wednesday

_____ / _____ / _____

Thursday

_____ / _____ / _____

Friday

_____ / _____ / _____

Saturday

_____ / _____ / _____

Sunday

_____ / _____ / _____

Notes

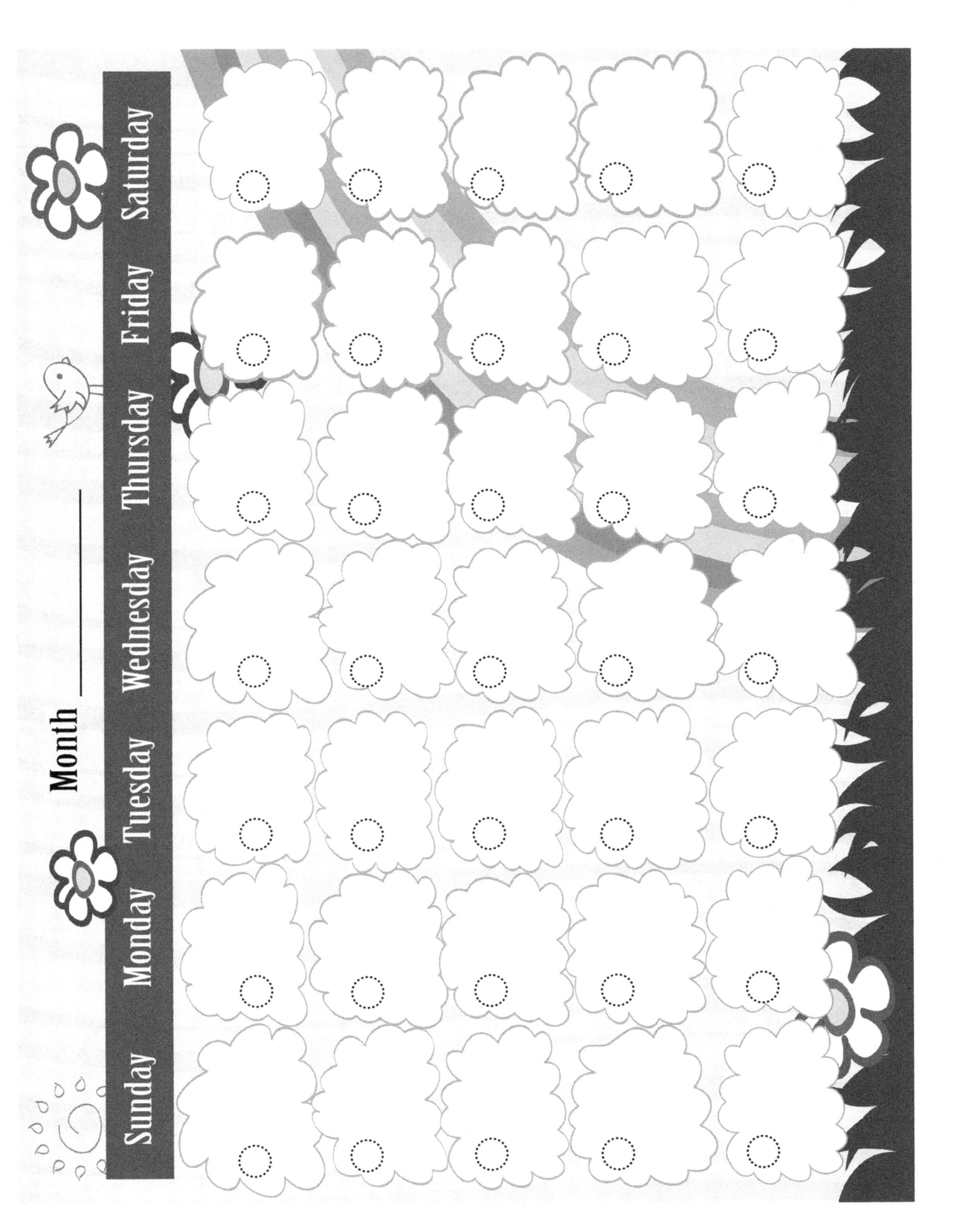

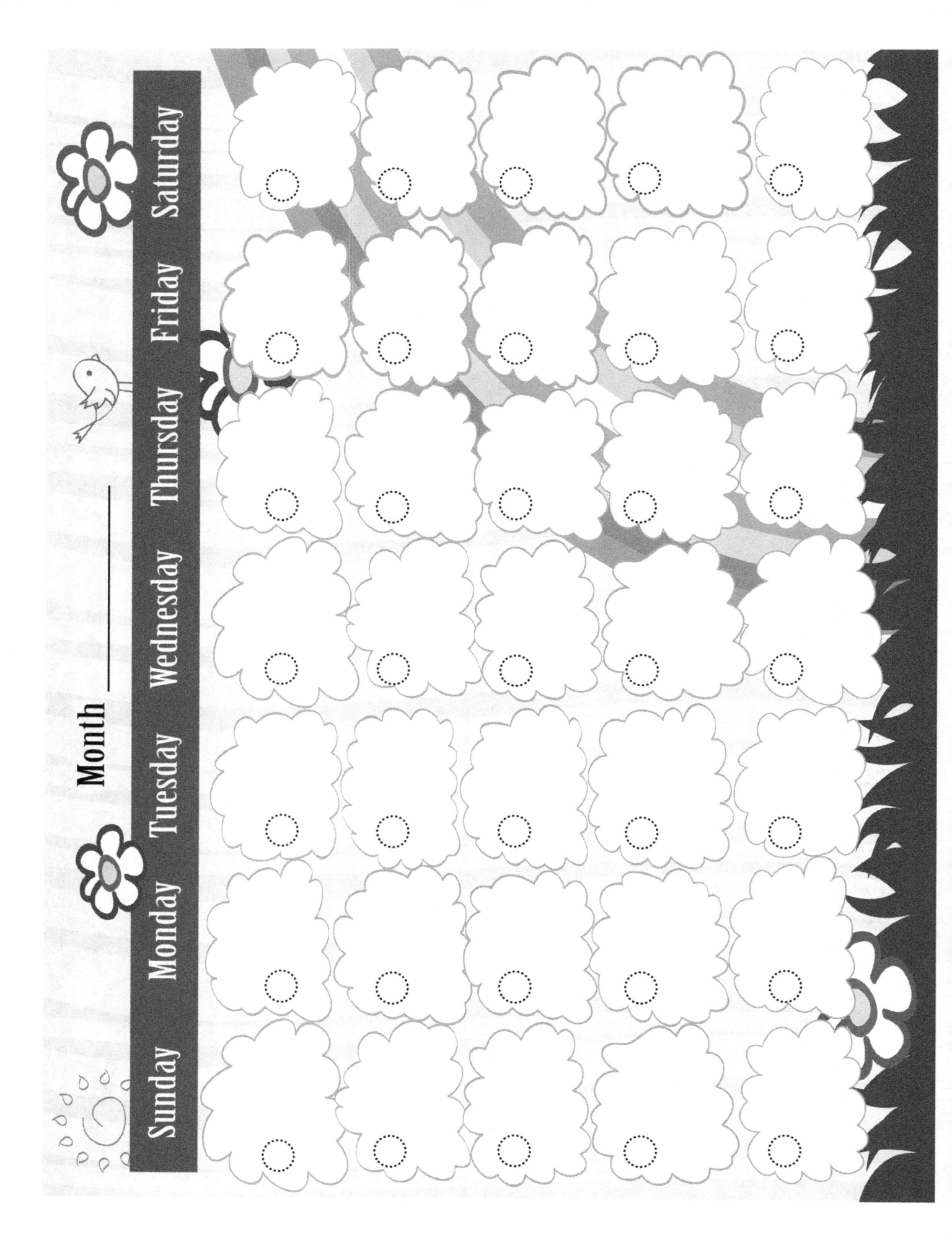

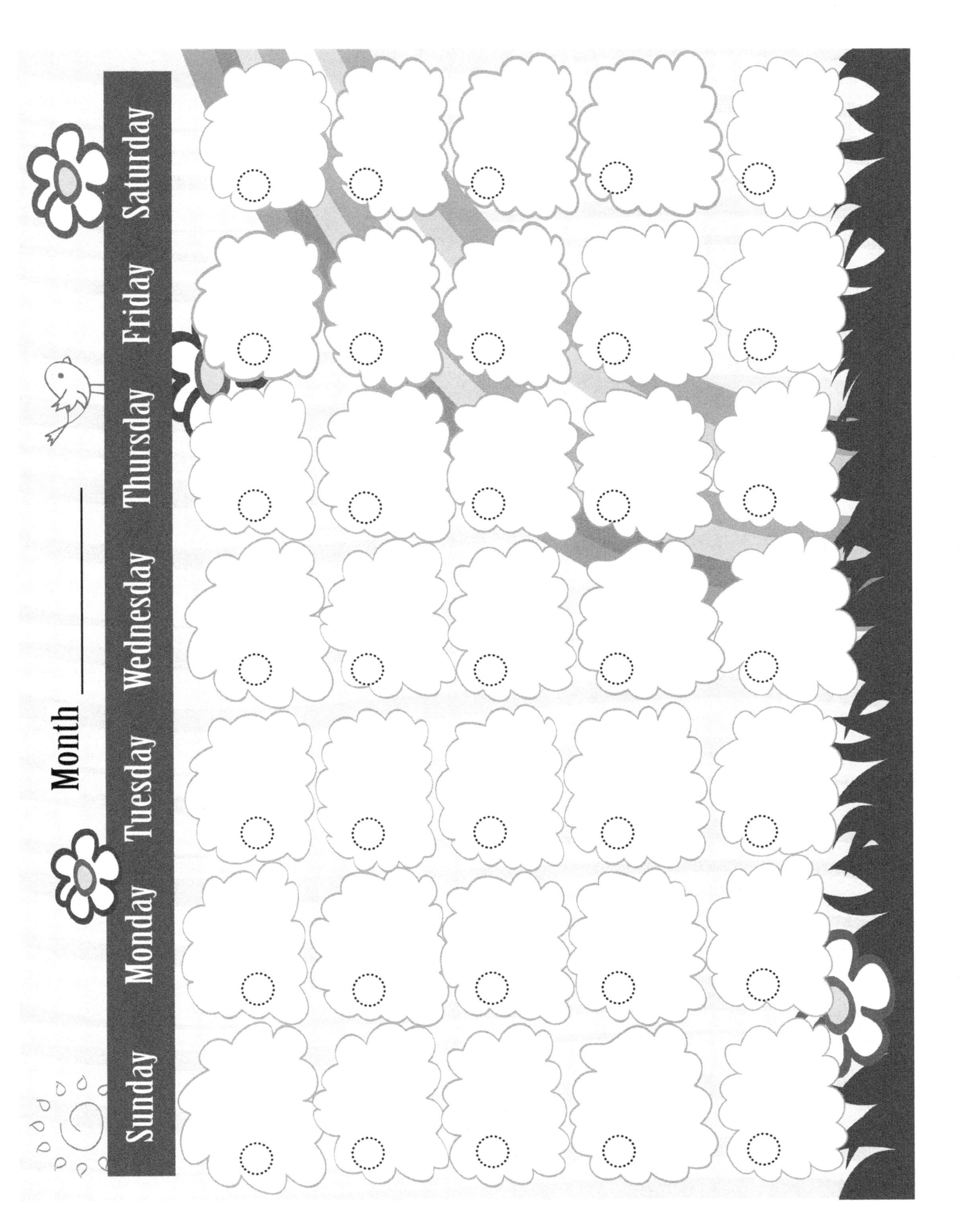

Made in the USA
Las Vegas, NV
16 January 2021